I0559869

DESPAIR TO JOY:

Recapture Peace, Confidence, and a Love for Life Through Trusting God

DEANVA STEPHEN

Kipekee Press
Ontario, Canada
www.kipekeepress.com

Cover and interior design by What's Your Story – Author Services

ISBN hardcover: 978-1-990728-20-4
ISBN paperback: 978-1-990728-19-8
ISBN ebook: 978-1-990728-21-1

DEDICATION

To women who may be on the path of losing,
or who already have lost, the hope of a joyful life.

CONTENTS

INTRODUCTION

Ephesians 2:10 NIV

For we are God's handiwork, created in Christ
Jesus to do good works, which God prepared
in advance for us to do.

This book is the testimony of a young lady named
Rose of how she lived a life in darkness encoun-
tering challenges upon challenges which
brought her grief upon grief. When she turned whole-
heartedly to God, her situation changed—first from
within. The intention of sharing this testimony is for
inspiring and encourages persons who encounter and
have encountered similar situations to know that they
can experience a life of fulfillment, which includes
unspeakable joy.

God created us in his image and likeness for His
pleasure. He gave us dominion over Earth and all the
living creatures. Due to Adam's and Eve's disobedience,

we lost this authority, and His Spirit departed from man, leading to the challenges and difficult situations some currently battle. Despite us committing wrong and making mistakes, He loves us unconditionally and made it possible for us to become righteous and live the glorious life He planned when He created us.

Rose's character was created to illustrate how if we choose to live without being connected to God, we are left to fight our battles on our own. When we do so, challenges and afflictions of this world beat us down before we find solutions, if they are ever found. Whereas when you are connected to God, when challenges and afflictions arise, you receive divine insight and direction from Holy Spirit. This helps to bring you out of the challenges without you being beaten down. At the moment the revelations my not make you feel good, but after they have resided in you, you will realise the revelations were for your good and are for you to uplift For instance, I created the character, Rose, to show how a person who goes through difficulties will have one experience without the support of God and another, once born again."

The death and resurrection of Jesus our Lord and Savior has made it possible to enter God's Kingdom. We see this through Rose: she believed in her heart that Jesus Christ is the Son of the living God. She believed that He died for her, and God raised Him from the dead and He's alive today. She confessed aloud, with her mouth, that

Jesus Christ is the Lord of her life. She also believed and confessed that through Him and in Him she is born again and has eternal life.

Having this faith, we are reborn by the Holy Spirit. We are propelled by the Holy Spirit to start living this new life; it is as if we are born anew and submitting ourselves to God completely. Submitting ourselves includes living according to His commands and principles. It doesn't matter which type of life you've lived prior to being born again; from the moment you accept Jesus into your heart you are a new creature.

Without Jesus, Rose lives a life of darkness facing tribulations and hardship and feeling there's no hope. Have you also felt this? Life challenges approach in all different categories: emotionally, physically, mentally, financially, and through poor health. In the midst of all these challenges, God sees you. However, you may continue to endure hardships and feel like there's no hope because you have not placed your trust and faith in Him, and you are seeking His purpose for you.

After accepting Christ as Lord and Savior along with living according to His commands, challenges will still arise. But when you do, after accepting Him, you ought to have no fear—being that you are now in Christ and an heir of God, you ought to prevail. The scriptures confirm that we who are of God have overcome them, because greater is He that is in us than he that is in the world. In Christ we have overcome them of this world (1 John 4:4). With this confirmation we recognize what we have and who we are. We now live by faith, having no fear because THE GREATER one dwells in us.

Our faith is manifested when tested. Hence, the scripture says count it all as joy when you go through diverse tests (James 1:2). Rose faces tests, too—just as we all do—and she has to reconfirm her faith many times. God loves His people living by faith in Him. The type of faith means that no matter how messy the situation may seem, you can trust that the end result will turn out for your good, simply because God favours you and He is able to do all things.

Perhaps you've been experiencing a certain challenge for a number of months: you don't give up on your faith in God. The bigger the challenge, the greater your testimony will be. Whatever difficult, painful, deep sorrow, heartbreak, abuse you may have endured or are enduring, as long as you are still walking the earth, you can change your story. You are capable of living a peaceful, righteous, happy, victorious, and purposeful eternal life.

We were all created with great purpose. Life on earth is time, time given to live God's purpose designed for us. It's sad that many leave the earth without fulfilling God's plan. The moment we accept him and follow our righteous heart's desire or the given vision by him that provides good to others we begin fulfilling his purpose for our life.

Some face continuous challenges in different areas of life: for, Rose, her challenge is the same as many young women her age—she is trying to find a partner to share her life with but keeps finding only those who are not trustworthy and who bring her down. Other types of challenges can include being indecisive on the type of work to pursue, or struggles with money. Others may know but face challenges with the appropriate connections, which contributes to setbacks. Perhaps unwise decisions were made at early stages of life. It can also be health challenge which create situations that seem hopeless. Thank God that regardless of how late or early you receive opportunities, from the moment you find God and receive salvation, you are on time. He restores what was lost or perhaps stolen. Regardless of how bad the health issues may seem, from the moment you receive salvation, you are cleansed; this brings healing and makes you divinely well. The scriptures confirm that He took up our infirmities and bore our diseases. (Mathew 8:17)

Some situations faced may leave you questioning your value, as they certainly did for Rose. You may feel like there is something wrong with you, you may feel you were not meant to experience lasting happiness. You may feel that you are being continually punished for poor decisions you made in the past. The great news is that with accepting Jesus as your Lord and living life abiding in him, these dark experiences and situations no longer have hold on you. You are now in the light. God is light!

God is able supply to all you require for life, but you first need to have that mentality. Your current or past experiences do not determine what's ahead unless you allow them to.

Some of us have behavioral faults, which we become more aware of when we start living according to God's word. God allows us to recognize them giving us a chance to correct them and move closer to becoming that perfect person He created us to be. The deeper we get in the word of God the more aware we become of unfavourable habits. With the mentality and drive to being a righteous person and efforts, we automatically start eliminating those undesirable habits. God's love and spirit in us give us the strength to perfect us.

PART I:

The Trials and Tribulations of Rose

CHAPTER ONE

Before I formed you in the womb I knew you,
before you were born I set you apart;
I appointed you as a prophet to the nations.

Jeremiah 1:5 NIV

Rose grew up in a small town on the outskirts of the capital city of a small Caribbean island. It was, at first, a happy home, one with both parents and five children. However, in the span of five years, when Rose was between the innocent and impressionable ages of twelve years and seventeen, she lost first a sister and then a brother. They both passed away suddenly. When Rose was twelve, her fourteen-year-old her sister lost consciousness and died. The family later found out it was due to a brain aneurysm. Her beloved older brother drowned when he was twenty-seven and Rose ten years younger. These deaths left a scar in the home and all of those who lived in it, including on Rose herself, her three remaining siblings, and their parents. Rose was devastated.

As a child, Rose enjoyed the company of older folks. It was easy for her to get the attention of visiting relatives who grew fond of her due to the attention she paid them; Rose was not shy to communicate with her older relatives. You would easily find her spending time with her grands. She did not hold back her thought when speaking. It was easier to be with older people, as Rose was also very defensive when teased and younger people tended to tease too much for Rose's liking.

Rose was also they child who was quick to try cooking. And even though the end results were not often palatable, she saw her potential as limitless. In school Rose was the type of person you would not want to get in an argument as she would just say whatever came to mind. Rose admired women in politics and wanted to be a government minister. Rose's outspokenness was unique amongst her siblings, who tended to be quieter and more reserved. Rose stood out from them because she questioned everything. As a child, her favourite word was "why." Being outspoken was not seen as a good characteristic in her family. Her inability to just accept things without question often led to argument with her parents, mostly her mother. Her mom pointed Rose out as the troublemaker as she would chat back when yelled at. Her family labeled her as rude.

Rose was never one to be stopped by rules or what people thought of her. So, when she was nineteen and met Jack, who was thirty-seven, she did not care if others were concerned about the age gap. She had just graduated from college and was, by all legal measures, a fully-grown woman. Jack was extremely charming and kind and treated her like a princess. He guided her without arguing with her, making her feel safe in his father-like presence. When he asked her to marry him, of course, she said yes.

CHAPTER TWO

Who saves me from my enemies.
You exalted me above my foes;
from a violent man you rescued me.

Psalms 18:48

To Rose, Jack was a hero; that he lavishly took care of her financial needs made her look up to him even more. She wanted to be with him all the time, so she moved out of her parents' house to live with Jack near town. Jack told her he fully supported her desire to go to university after they got married, even offering to pay the tuition fee. Rose was pleased to get away from the doom of loss surrounding her parents' home. Her new life with Jack seemed was full of possibility.

A few months after moving in with her, Jack's character changed rapidly—to a point that Rose did not even recognise the man she was with. Gone was the Jack who loved to discuss their future and who valued her intelligence. In his place was a man who did not want to hear her opinions; in fact, she was not *allowed* to voice her opinion in situations if they differed from his. The moment she tried Jack would snap at her.

Whenever Rose stepped out to do errands, he wanted to be there, too. He did not want her going into town unless he was with her. Rose signed up for classes at a gym near the house, which made him furious. One afternoon, Rose went to the gym while Jack was at work but did not inform him. Jack called her cellphone during the gym session and when she stepped outside to take the call, she realised Jack was outside of the gym waiting for her, furious she hadn't asked his permission ahead of time. This was an absolute different man from the Jack that Rose had agreed to marry, the man she fell in love with.

He became even more controlling and would not allow her to search for a job. She realized that her dream of going to university would have to be abandoned. And the abuse was not only emotional and mental, but also physical. One evening, when they were driving home late at night after spending some time with other couples, a minor disagreement was turning into something major simply because Jack did not like that Rose disagreed with him. Rose did not want to find out where his upset could lead, as she noticed the change in his facial expression and knew that his increasing anger was dangerous. She did everything to deescalate the situation. She hoped that by simply agreeing with him and saying very little, Jack would calm down. Instead, he was getting more and more angry.

When the vehicle approached a stoplight, Rose tried as hard as she could to sound calm; she asked Jack to let her leave. Instead, he grabbed her by the hair to prevent her from jumping out of the car. He drove into an isolated area in woods near the beach and parked. Reaching under his seat, he grabbed a machete and placed it near her throat.

"You always want to make me look stupid. I'm ready to shut you up for good," he said. Rose felt the cold steel metal press into her skin; she felt she was living what could be her last breaths. She looked at Jack and no longer recognized him as the man who used to look at her with softness. His eyes were on the machete and his hand was steady as he pressed the machete with growing force against her neck.

"I'm sorry! I'm sorry!" she repeated, trying to reach the old Jack but he was like a robot. His eyes were glazed, so committed in what he said he was planning to do. Rose saw no way out and resigned herself to death. *This is it*, she thought.

Suddenly, a vehicle pulled up beside them and three men with rifles approached their car. Jack quickly pulled away and put the machete back under his seat. Rose saw it was a group of police officers doing a spot check.

"What are you doing stopped around here, so deep in the woods this time of night?" They shone flashlights into their faces and into the back seat, checking to see who was with us.

One of the officers asked if everything was okay. Rose was still in tears. "Are you okay?" the officer asked again, looking only at Rose. Convinced that even if the officers saved her from her immediate situation that Jack would find her and hurt her if she said "no," Rose replied, "I'm fine."

The officer continued to hold her gaze until Rose dropped her eyes. She heard their footsteps as they left and headed back to their cars. Jack waited until they drove away then accused her of dialling 911 while he was driving.

"No, I didn't call anyone!" Rose responded, as she had not: she was telling the truth. Eventually Jack cooled off and they drove home.

Despite it being against Jack's wishes, Rose had wanted to secure job in order to contribute money towards the wedding. She felt that once she got one, he might lighten up, especially after she explained why she wanted to work. She applied to few places and was granted an interview. After the first interview she received a call for a second interview. This time she felt the need to share her plans with Jack. He was not pleased that she was trying to get a job. She figured that his response was based on his concern that a job would making her more independent so she tried to convince him that the only reason for the job was to save for their wedding.

"You want a job so you can wear high heels in town, so other men can see you," he said, and then he called her all kinds of vile names.

Rose felt trapped in a prison, that her relationship was beyond a nightmare. Jack would sleep out two to three nights a week claiming he had to work late or had to travel for work. When Rose brought up questions, since she suspected he was being dishonest, he would get violent.

Rose did not want her family or anyone to know what was going on in her home. Her pride and fear of Jack kept her silent. She also felt ashamed to share the brutal abuse she was experiencing. Plus, if during an altercation at the house she felt helpless and cried out for help he would get more furious and hurt her more. *Imagine what he would do if he found out I told anyone?* she thought.

After numerous life threating scenarios, including getting her nose badly bruised and having hot coffee thrown over her face, Rose realised the only suitable option for her getting away from Jack was leaving the country. She had tried and failed to leave him. The island was too small to hide in. He did not want her to leave him despite how much he appeared to despise her. He would not stop the abuse and life threating actions yet in the next breath, he'd claim he was sorry and that he loved her.

With the help of a friend who had seen the bruises and would not let Rose get away with saying "I'm okay", Rose made it onto a plane to Canada. It was the only way to escape the abuse and death threats. She held her breath as passengers entered and the plane readied for take-off. She was terrified Jack would somehow find out where she was and push his way on the plane, that he would successfully drag her off and embarrass her. She feared what would happen if she ended up back home with him.

She relaxed only when the plane touched down in Canada. She was only twenty years old and on her own, far from all she knew.

CHAPTER THREE

Though we experience every kind of pressure,
we're not crushed. At times we don't know
what to do, but quitting is not an option.

2 Corinthians 4:8 TPT

Rose sought out her grandfather who lived in a rural area of Canada. She had never physically met him and he was happy to see her. He did not ask many questions and she did not tell him she had escaped from her abusive ex-fiancé. The "why" of her arrival did not matter to him. After some time with her grandfather, Rose went to visit an aunt she had spoken with prior to her trip. After some time in the city of Toronto where her aunt resided, Rose decided city life would be better for her. However, staying with her aunt wasn't an option because her aunt's boyfriend was aggressive in his attempts to get her into his bed.

Rose was in Canada on a one- year tourist visa. If she didn't go back, then automatically her status would change to one of an immigrant without residence documents. When the approved stay time was up, she had to choose between staying in Canada or going back to her home island. She heard from family members how outraged Jack was that she'd left him: going home would mean she would be right back where she started—living in fear and knowing that the chances of being murdered by her abusive ex-fiancé were too high to discount.

She decided to stay in Canada for her safety.

For the first eighteen months she worked at a duck processing plant. The odour and temperature of the environment were barely tolerable and Rose wished she did not have to go there. However, Rose could not afford to be picky. There were not many choices for her since as she had expenses and no work documents. Employment opportunities for her were scarce so she had to keep her job at the duck processing plant.

Rose thought back to some of the happier times of her childhood. She was brought up attending Catholic Church, but at the age of fifteen, she and her family began attending a Pentecostal church. She had not fully committed her life to Christ and was living the life similar to a non-believer. The interest and urge to attend church regularly were in her, but she used the excuse of there being no churches near her home; she ignored the urges. She made no effort to seek support from the church.

After a year of grieving her previous years of abuse, Rose was lonely and decided she would seek out a partner. She figured that if she took things slowly and dated casually, she would find the right person, get married, and become legally established in Canada. With that, she could return to school and in due time start a family. But that is not what happened. For years, Rose experienced disappointment after disappointment. Most of the men she dated were mainly after fun and would use all sorts of lies to trick her into sex and informal companionship. Men who were already in relationships claimed they were single.

She planned that someday, after being married, she would commit to living in line with God's principles. In the meantime, most of her weekends were spent alone in her room crying. Being alone and away from her family was one thing, but Rose also had to watch over her shoulders due to the fear of being sent back to the island—the island where she would have to watch over her shoulders due to Jack.

Loneliness filled her heart. She felt relieved that she was away from Jack, but she was not happy with how her life was going. Waking up before the crack of dawn, then travelling over two hours to the duck farm was not fun. However, it was the only way to pay her bills and it was also necessary because she had no documents which would allow her to find a different job. For years this was her life. In the midst it all she always called to God for strength and guidance.

Rose spent years working in factories for minimum cash payment and she had many failed attempts to build relationships. Most of the "better" men were looking for women who were established and not someone who was working on it. Often, she looked at herself in the mirror and whispered to her reflection, *"What's wrong with you? Why can't you find happiness? Why can't you find that person who will accept you and love you unconditionally? Why is it that the men who approach you are mainly out for fun?*

CHAPTER FOUR

*Dear friends, do not believe every spirit, but test
the spirits to see whether they are from God,
because many false prophets have
gone out into the world.*

1John 4:1 NIV

Four years later, at age twenty-five, Rose moved and was happy to discover a gospel church near her new home. She attended service regularly on Sunday mornings. The regular praise and worship gave her strength; she began feeling hopeful for her future, about her life. But after a few months, Rose relocated to a place without a nearby church. Although she promised herself she would make the effort to attend the previous gospel church she enjoyed, she used cold winter mornings as an excuse to stay home. Instead, of getting out of bed on Sunday mornings, she would snuggle deeper into her warm bed and go back to sleep.

Her employer made changes which included a lower wage for the staff in her department. Since the changes had been incorporated, the team she worked with stopped some of their cleaning duties. However, her direct manager at the plant did not understand that the decision was made by a few people and not the whole department. The truth and the initial act of reducing their wages did not matter to that manager. He decided to fire the entire team.

Hearing her supervisor break the news felt like she was being punched in the gut. Rose could see no light in the situation. No one to turn to, huge bills to pay, and with no work permit, Rose was desperate. Rose started a job search by all possible means available to her— through agencies, job postings, and she even placed her own ads online hoping that an employer who paid cash would reach out.

Weeks went by turning into months and nothing came up. Her meagre savings were running out. She prayed, but her faith was weak as she felt hopeless. She was praying but she did not have faith that God could help her out of this dark phase. She received few responses regarding employment and none of them were legit. She feared that she eventually she would have zero dollars. Rose fell into depression.

There was one interesting response to her search for work from a gentleman named Manny; he said he was an investor. He reached out to Rose about an investment proposal. It entailed her receiving a loan with his connections and investing in a house flipping project. New houses were being flipped and sold within three months. He explained she would receive more than double of the investment. It all seemed too sketchy. Rose refused the offer. But Manny was persistent.

After sitting down with Manny, Rose felt she had no choice but to take a chance. She accepted the proposal. He processed the application, and as he'd claimed, she did receive a loan of $5000. As agreed, she immediately transferred the money into his account. The agreement was that every other week during the three months the house was being renovated, Manny would pay the loan and once the house was sold, the loan would be paid off with the proceeds and Rose would receive a significant return on her investment.

Manny made the first couple of payments but as the date of the third payment approached, Rose had a difficult time tracking him. He was not returning calls, text messages, or emails. Rose started to panic. The entire day the loan payment was due went by with not a word from Manny. Rose was forced to dip into her small remaining bit of savings to make the payment.

The weekend went by with no response from Manny despite the hundreds of times Rose tried reaching him. Anxiety engulfed her. Unemployment with living expenses plus now she was left to pay a loan? She tried to stay positive and kept believing Manny would reach out with the funds.

Weeks went by and he did not deliver. When she finally got a word from him, he claimed they were having issues with the investment. At this point Rose did not care about returns on investment, she simply wanted out of the agreement. She wanted the funds returned just for paying off the loan so she would be out of the situation. Manny was being difficult and claimed the money was tied up and he had no access to it.

He had obviously scammed her. Rose had entered the agreement and didn't even have any signed documents. She had trusted this man and he had left her paying a bi-weekly loan in the midst of her unemployment. He knew she was not employed, yet he led her into a worse situation. Bills were piling up and Rose was running out of funds. She felt out of options, but then she spotted one: nanny and housekeeping jobs.

Rose eventually got accepted as a live-in nanny for two boys in a rural area east of the city. With this job, she would only be at the apartment she rented for two weekends in a month, so she ended the lease and planned on staying with a close cousin when she was away from her live-in job.

Then nanny job was a fail: her working hours were extended with no increase in the already very low wage.

After working for a couple weeks, Rose left as the nanny job wasn't even covering her expenses. Back at her cousin's place she went back into job hunting and thankfully, got hired as a cashier at a small grocery store.

With the security of the job, she enrolled in a French course at a local university. She knew this would be an asset in applying for her resident documents. Things were turning around for Rose. She felt back in control of her life. She was thankful to God for bringing her out of the distress.

Then one Tuesday morning, a colleague picked her up to go to work and just as the car was about to take off, police officers surrounded it. In shock and suspense as to why police would surround them, they all stayed calm and waited for the police to approach the car. Surprisingly, the one who did addressed Rose. He introduced himself as an immigration officer and requested her ID.

CHAPTER FIVE

*Have I not commanded you? Be strong and
courageous. Do not be afraid; do not be dis-
couraged, for the LORD your God will be with
you wherever you go.*

Joshua 1:9 NIV

R ose seized up for a few seconds. She handed
over her ID. The officer informed her that he
would be taking her into a detention centre
since she had been living illegally in Canada. The rest of
the people in the car were allowed to continue to work.
On the way to detention, Rose discovered that it was
Manny who had reported her to immigration. Not only
had he scammed her into a debt of $5000, now he was
trying to have her deported.

As she rode to the detention centre with the officers, the thought of what could happen next flooded
her mind. Rose knew that going back to her home island

was not an option. Her fear of her ex-fiancé was even more powerful than any worry about being detained.

The environment at the detention centre was dreary. The section where Rose held was occupied with many other women detained for various reasons. It was not officially a prison, but it certainly felt and operated like one. Rose spent two sleepless nights there, worried about what she could do with the current situation. She had no appetite and was unable to sleep. She knew that by this point the abuse she had experienced back home was out in the open. Many people knew what she had suffered. She hoped that would be enough evidence to prove her life was in danger if she returned. That known risk could be the only way she might be permitted to stay in Canada and be protected from her ex. Rose was released on bond. Thankfully her grandfather came through with the funds.

Rose being exposed to immigration forced her to file for status as a legal resident rather than her plan to find someone who would marry her so she could stay. Rose knew the only way she'd have a chance at permanent residency was to be honest about the true reason she migrated to Canada. She had to trust God to deliver her.

Rose was officially not allowed to work. Although before she had been caught, she was working illegally for cash, she could no longer risk even looking for work.

It felt like the load of pressure and stress was getting heavier. She had been independent from the time she migrated to Canada until now. She was helpless and living with her cousin. Communication with God and believing He was hearing was her only comfort in the darkness of her situation. Rose gave herself over to God was deeper in prayer than ever before. She knew that God rescued her from Jack that time in the woods and had helped her get to Canada. She trusted God would not put her back where he could hurt her. That belief gave her strength and changed her despair to hope.

At the first meeting with her legal counsel, when asked what she planned on doing, Rose explained her reason migrating. She found some comfort when the lawyer confirmed that abuse was a solid defence and it could be a cause for receiving residency and protection. The challenge was having the judge believe her story of her two years relationship with Jack and all the terrible life-threating experiences he put her through. Unfortunately, she had to relive the horror by documenting her abusive experiences in detail.

Her life had change to the point she felt like she was just occupying space and spent all her time worrying, day after day. Her dress size went down from a size ten to a size six. There was a nasty feeling in her head that lingered all day and night. She was unable to fall asleep yet she only wanted to be in bed under the sheets.

Rose pushed herself into praying earnestly; she had to have faith that her prayers would be answered. At the time, Rose had just started dating Derek. They met at the grocery store where she previously worked. As she had to quit the job and she felt so low, she sought any connection, so despite not knowing him very well or for very long, she opened up and explained what was going on. Derek was moved by her story and told her he did not want her to be sent back to her home country where she could be killed by Jack. He was concerned that the courts would nake a mistake and not see her need for protection. Derek was a Canadian citizen and knew of one way he could help her: he offered to marry her. Just in case the courts did not believe Rose needed protection, Derek would do so by sponsoring her as his wife. Rose was surprised and relieved. She thanked God and started seeing light in her challenges.

Derek was a born-again Christian and had trusted Rose when she told him that she was ready to receive salvation and live her life in way that was pleasing God. Rose had confessed the Lordship of Jesus in the past, and prayed to Him in the present, but had never committed herself fully to Christianity. Now was the time to do so.

Rose felt the happiest she had been in years. She had finally met her future husband, and he was a

Christian who wanted her to join him in a life dedicated to Christ. It was like her prayers were being answered in a way she did not believe possible. In the midst of all her distress, Derek who was ready to call her his wife. *Wow wow wow*! She felt joy pass over her like a cool breeze on a hot day over her. Rose was in awe of her good fortune. She felt valued and thanked God for his blessings.

They immediately began making wedding arrangements—planning a date and making a list of who to invite. Derek and Rose got to know more about each other while planning the wedding and this is where Rose became fearful about what she was getting into. While Rose spent more time at Derek's house, which would soon be her home, she noticed disturbing characteristics in him.

Rose was caught off guard when Derek designed the wedding band he wanted Rose to get him. It was no ordinary wedding band: he wanted top of the line. Rose was not able afford the exact style but she tried to get him one as similar as possible. It felt overwhelming to plan a wedding within a short period—and more so as Derek left all the expenses to Rose.

Rose was aching to ask him why he was not contributing but she chose to keep quiet and work with it. After all, she was happy that he had arrived just when she needed him. She was slightly turned off by him requiring her to cover all the expenses, but she assumed he was not financially stable at the time and decided to be patient and understanding.

One evening while Rose gently asked Derek questions about his finances, he opened up and shared he was not in a great place financially due to filing bankruptcy on a bookstore he had opened with his ex. Derek shared that his ex-girlfriend had taken all the proceeds and left the expenses to him. This left him with a bad credit record.

Rose's heart melted when Derek shared this with her. She hugged him and said it would all be alright. Rose, being experienced with people taking advantage over others financially, felt compassion for Derek. Suddenly the fact he was having her cover all the wedding expenses was not a big issue to her. She looked at the positive: she would be married and that her husband-to-be was a man of God.

Rose came from a French-speaking background and spoke in French to relatives over the phone. One morning while Rose was on the phone with an aunt, Derek walked in. Rose cut the conversation short since he did not understand French and she did not want to appear rude by speaking a language that she knew Derek did not understand.

Derek gave her an odd look. "Why did you get off the phone so fast? Who were you speaking to?"

"My aunt," Rose replied. She was unaware that Derek did not believe her.

As the wedding date got loser, Rose felt Derek was no longer acting like he wanted to be with her. He would get up from the couch if she approached and he would answer her questions with only one word or with grunts, sometimes even with eyerolls. He avoided eye contact and rarely started conversations with her. Rose asked him why his behaviour towards her had changed. He responded that he did not trust her due to the phone call he walked in on. She was communicating in a foreign language with *someone*, and he didn't believe it was an aunt. His instincts were telling him not to marry her, he said.

Words aren't enough to describe what came over Rose after hearing Derek speak those words. She couldn't understand, nor could she make sense of, what was taking place. Things just kept switching constantly in her life. She went from despairing to joy in an instant; now with his words, she feared that she was heading back to depression. Rose was speechless for a little while, just trying to absorb it. It was like she received a dose of what happiness and her future could be, then it was suddenly to vanish due to Derek's insecurity.

Rose pleaded with Derek, trying to convince him of her transparency. She wanted them to get to know more of each other as husband and wife with God in the center. She explained that most communications with her relatives are in their native French language. She reminded him that he was not there when she got on the phone with her aunt and assured him that she did not intend to speak in a language he didn't know in his presence, and that is why she cut the conversation short so abruptly.

Her words rekindled feelings in Derek's heart and he apologized for his overreaction, explaining he did not want to make a mistake in getting married. He apologized for his drastic change of mind and, with that, announced that the wedding was back on. However, Rose was not overly happy. She began having doubts that she could rely on his word. She feared he might not show up on their wedding day.

On the morning of the wedding, Rose woke feeling dread that she was making the wrong decision. This was not how she wanted to feel on her wedding day. She took a deep breath to calm herself and decided that after the wedding took place there would be less distractions and she and Derek would focus on their relationship. Yes, there were questions and a lot she did not know about him, but they had a lifetime to make things work.

CHAPTER SIX

The LORD will fight for you;
you need only to be still.

Exodus 14:14 NIV

It was sunny, beautiful day when Rose and Dereck got married at Toronto's City Hall with a handful of people in attendance, all dressed elegantly to celebrate the occasion. After the civil ceremony, they went out to an Asian restaurant for a scrumptious lunch and Derek and Rose continued to celebrate all week. On the following weekend, Rose and Dereck hosted a dinner party where they cut their wedding cake and friends toasted to their future. Rose felt extremely grateful that in the midst of the darkness going on in her life, God had given her a husband—a husband who was born again and actively engaged in church. She was determined to have a successful marriage.

Dereck had a cheerful personality; he liked dancing, singing, being well-dressed, and cooking. He was also very tidy and kept his surrounding organised. Rose too keeps her surrounding tidy and organized so that part of Dereck attracted her. However, Rose was worried as she noticed some red flags—behaviours in her new husband which suggested he was struggling to affirm his commitment to her. For instance, if Rose used any groceries he had purchased, he expected her to replace them, particularly if it was anything he had purchased before she moved in. Derek would have her pay the bill without contributing when they dined out. He knew her situation, including the added burden of her lawyer fees, but he paid no mind to it and put additional financial stresses on her. In addition, he did not invite her to his church, he had not introduced her to his kids, and he did not wear his wedding band unless they went out together.

Derek was intensely passionate and wanted to explore a variety of sexual activities Rose was not familiar or comfortable with. She never expected after they got married, he would have such adventurous requests of her. It was an unexpected side of him which shocked her. When she expressed her discomfort, he kept reminded her that she was his wife; he insisted that she was obligated to satisfy his needs.

The elevation of attraction she anticipated towards Derek was just not happening. She married him despite not feeling physically attracted to him and, on top of that, she found many of his emerging characteristics unappealing. She began resisting him as she couldn't hide her discomfort. They were totally different in what they expected from each other financially and in bed. She made the effort to co-operate and meet him halfway, but he would not do the same for her. Rather than becoming closer, they were becoming increasingly distant.

One evening Rose got home early and surprised Derek who was on video call with a female who, from her quick glance at the screen, was lying in bed. When he saw Rose enter, he immediately ended the call.

"Who is she?" Rose asked.

"A friend," he replied and ended the conversation. However, that night the house phone rang constantly and Derek would not answer it. Rose did not yet feel comfortable answering his phone and the constantly ringing phone was odd because neither of them addressed it.

Since he refused to pick up, Rose was able to make a mental note of the number. She then wrote the caller's number down in her phone. She recognized the area code as Jamaican, Derek's place of birth. Whoever was calling did not live in Canada, so that gave Rose some confidence.

A couple days after this stressful weekend, Derek told Rose his daughters would be coming for the weekend and wanted to spend some time alone with them. He needed to borrow her house key to give his daughters access while he was still out. She handed him her keys to the apartment and made plans to spend that weekend at her cousin's place. On Monday afternoon, as she was getting ready to go back to the marital home, she received a text from Derek stating he no longer wanted to be with her. He made it clear she was not to go back to their home.

This struck Rose full force, like a speeding bulldozer. She figured Derek was having a moment of mental illness as she could not process his devasting message. They had only been married for a few weeks, but Rose tried not to panic as she considered Derek's behavior in regards to the French conversation with her aunt before the wedding. That time, after they sat together and spoke about it, he had taken back his idea of breaking up. But she was also wondering about the woman she saw him on video call with. She worried that woman was the reason he wanted to end their marriage. She also thought back to Derek saying that he had gotten close to a woman while on vacation in Jamaica, but things had not worked out. Rose rushed to the apartment hoping she and Derek could have a conversation to resolve the issue.

On arrival at the apartment, Derek would not let her in. He told her to go away and that he did not want to see or speak with her. After knocking on the apartment door for over an hour, Rose realized that he was actually serious and would not change his mind. Immediately, she fell to the ground and anxiety came upon her.

Here, in the midst of her immigration crisis she got married, thinking that would resolve it. And now, only three weeks into the marriage he started treating her like some girl who was a casual fling? Her stomach sank as she leaned on the wall. Had she dug a deeper and darker hole for herself in her rush to marriage? She got up to continue knocking. After three hours of trying to get Derek to open the door and talk to her, Rose left.

Derek blocked her cell number, refusing to communicate. This commenced another episode of tearful and sleepless nights for Rose. She felt like she had no strength, not even after praying. She slept fitfully and upon waking, could not get up. She spent entire days in bed. She felt like she had lost herself; she did not feel like her normal being. She could not even remember what that was to feel normal and to have normal things happen to her. Her life was just a series of grief and disappointments.

She had lost her independence; her cousin allowed her to stay with her out of concern. For years Rose had been on her own, paying her bills and maintaining a livelihood. From the moment she lost her job at the duck factory, things declined, descending like a rollercoaster. Would there ever be a stable light in her affairs?

Rose reached out to God for help as she felt only He could bring her out of this storm. Again, she became persistent in prayer. Despite her efforts, Derek would not change his mind. Rose gave up and began putting all her faith in God to lead her out of her confusing situation. Praying became a constant in her life. She knew the only way to get what she sought was by asking God.

CHAPTER SEVEN

*So do not fear, for I am with you; do not be
dismayed, for I am your God. I will strengthen
you and help you; I will uphold you with my
righteous right hand.*

Isaiah 41:10

Rose resumed staying at her cousin, Leah's, house. Leah was having her own problems. She was in a ten-year relationship with a married man and had a son with him. His wife found out, and her boyfriend left Leah to save his marriage.

One evening, Leah's married ex-boyfriend called Rose asking if she could meet him and drop off some documents for Leah. Rose agreed, thinking she was doing some good. That evening Leah was out. On her return Rose handed her the documents, explaining that she had got the documents to save her the trouble.

Rose was expecting gratitude from Leah; however, what she received was the opposite.

Leah was upset that Rose had picked up the documents, saying at very least, her ex should have had to pay someone to dropped them off. Instead, he handed them over through Rose for free. She was insulted and angry. As her rage grew, there was no one to turn on but Rose.

"So, all this time, you were on *his* side, yet you are living in my house for free?" Leah's anger engulfed her and there was no way Rose could reason with her. Leah demanded that Rose leave her house.

Rose's initial plan was to go to a hotel, then she remembered her friend Elise, a former co-worker at the duck factory, had just moved into a new home and that it was nearby. God's work is mysterious—by coincidence it would seem, Rose had actually spoken with Elise that very day, so she messaged her informing her what was going on. Without even hearing the full story, Elise suggested she stay with her and offered to pick her up right away. "I'll be there in ten minutes," Elise promised, and she was. Rose praised God as she got into Elise's car. What was a huge relief to not have to find a hotel.

Rose was grateful that Elise was so willing to welcome her into her new home she had just purchased with her boyfriend, Brian. Rose again was feeling dizzy due to the sudden turns in her fortune. She didn't not understand what had just happened. Along with all what she was facing, she was now homeless. She did not know what to do next. She had no one to turn to with her situation besides Elise who kept assuring her that she would help her.

Rose felt like the was no hope for her as it was Leah who had signed her bond and assured immigration that she would be responsible for her. Now Leah had kicked her out. Praying and communicating with God was the only thing that gave Rose strength. She believed that through God things would be alright.

Elise ran a spa and did the bookings from home via phone. She asked Rose to help with the client bookings since she was at the house. It seemed like a great opportunity for Rose, at least at first. She would not have to leave the house while her rent was covered, plus she'd earn some pocket change. Later, Rose drove Brian's truck to Leah's place where she and Elise grabbed all her belongings while Leah was at work.

Rose discovered a beautiful ministry nearby and resumed going to church each Sunday. While in church praising, praying, and worshipping God, she allowed hope to bloom in her. She knew that she was not living according to the commands of God, but she had faith that God was hearing her when she spoke to Him.

Rose was waiting for the response of her refugee claim. When one evening Rose received a text from Leah stating there was a mail for her from immigration,

Rose knew that it was the verdict from her claim. She immediately went over to collect her mail. Although anxiety and fear had covered her, Rose waited until she was back at her new home before she opened the envelope. She tore open the envelop and read that her claim for protection had been denied.

Although the news was disappointing it did not come as a shock to Rose since her lawyer had advised her it was possible. The lawyer had also told her they would immediately go to Plan B, which was to get the case appealed.

As the weeks and months went by Rose, worked on her divorce from Derek, appealing her refugee case with immigration, as well as on developing a stronger connection with God. She had become excited about attending church on Sunday mornings, even making effort to attend Sunday evening services. The pastor at that church preached remarkably well; after every service Rose felt stronger in faith. Through the services and prayer, she reinforced her hope things would turn out in her favour.

On a Sunday morning while Rose was in church, she reflected on her life and the fact that she was not living the life of a born-again Christian. When she was a young girl, she had recited the prayer of salvation, but she never lived the life of a devoted Christian. She was not living according to God's commands and principles.

Rose had that desire to live righteous and according to God's laws, but with her current situation it would have been difficult to keep that commitment.

While standing in service in the midst of prayer, Rose called out to God, asking for Him to makes a change in the situation so she could receive her landed immigration status. Rose also promised to give her life to Christ and live a righteous life.

Now it's been said that you should not bargain in this way—make a request of God promising to live according to His will only if He delivers. At the moment Rose did not know better; she was in a desperate situation and knew only God could turn things in her favor. So, she said that prayer and had faith God heard.

CHAPTER EIGHT

Even though I walk through the darkest valley,
I will fear no evil, for you are with me; your rod
and your staff, they comfort me.

Psalm 23:4 NIV

Rose and Elise had developed a close relationship as they lived together. Elise was very supportive with Rose's situation but over the last few months they had been living together, Elise had begun acting funny, like a kindergarten kid. Rose asked her what was going on. What there something wrong? Elise responded that as a teenager she was diagnosed with a mental disorder which caused her to behave like a five-year-old certain times. Although Rose had never heard of such a condition, she squashed any doubts she felt about the explanation. She had compassion for Elise and did her best to be there for her as much as she could, helping her however and whenever she was able.

But a second discovery made her even more wary of Elise's sometimes odd behaviour. *Could it be drugs?* Rose thought, then immediately dismissed the suggestions each time they came up in her mind. She could not afford to question things. Rose realized the spa Elise was running wasn't offering the types of services a typical spa did. It did not offer beauty treatments to women, it was actually offering massages to men. Rose had no choice but to accept Elise's explanations and excuses about the types of services she was helping to procure, as she needed the accommodation Elise provided as well as the money she received for answering the phones.

By chance, Rose met a gentleman named Marco who showed great interest in dating. He was a welcome distraction from her concerns. Initially, she did not feel attracted to him when he approached her, but after a brief chat she accepted his number. It was nice to have male attention and it took her mind off Elise, her job, her upcoming-divorce, and her immigration problems. Marco was in town for business and was headed back to his home in Montreal, however, he knew business would bring him back to Toronto quite soon.

Marco liked her, and Rose was flattered when he insisted she meet him for dinner in a couple of weeks. She didn't dive into calling or messaging him right away, since she was not attracted to him. A few weeks went by, and Rose didn't call or text. However, one evening while chilling and scrolling through social media on her phone, she felt compelled to messaged Marco to say hi.

He responded with joy; he said he'd been waiting to hear from her. They started to text regularly and also got into some lengthy conversations, getting acquainted and sharing their life stories. Marco invited Rose to an event his social group was hosting in Montreal. Rose accepted and visited Montreal the following weekend.

Marco was quite the gentleman. When Rose arrived at the train station, he greeted her warmly and lead her to a restaurant for lunch. While they were there, Marco received a call from his friend, Antonio, who lived in the in the United States. He asked to greet Rose on the telephone. Rose was quite flattered that Marco's friend wanted to say hello to her. She spoke briefly with Antonio who was pretty nice. Marco booked Rose into a hotel and reimbursed the train fare. The following day Rose returned to Toronto having spent a good evening in downtown Montreal.

After many conversations, Rose and Marco began dating. His personality attracted her despite the lack of physical spark, at least on her side. She was also intrigued by his best-friend, Antonio. Marco did not like Rose's frequent questions about Antonio, but when pressed, he still showed her a photo of the two of them in front of a touristy spot in New York City. Rose felt guilty; she admitted to herself that she felt an intense attraction to Antonio which she could not dismiss despite the fact that Antonio and Marco were best friends.

She and Marco spoke often, and Rose opened up and shared what was going on in her life. He was compassionate towards her and the challenges. As weeks went by, she and Marco met up in different cities where he travelled for work. The weekend Marco was planning on visiting Rose in Toronto, he received a call that his brother in the States was ill and instead travelled there. While Marco was in the States he communicated with Rose via Antonio's phone since they were together and were he to use his Canadian phone, it would incur expensive roaming charges. Rose also spoke with Antonio independently of Marco, as he now had her phone number.

Marco was much older than Rose and felt the need to have an opinion in all decisions she made. Rose was used to making all her decisions solo and after her experience with Jack, she was wary of older men trying to control her. That was a challenge for her and Marco. And then Antonio began calling Rose occasionally to say hi. Rose wondered if he shared an attracted to her. Marco had told her Antonio was single and was recovering from a breakup with a girlfriend.

After three months of dating, Rose and Marco decided to go their separate ways. Marco made a comment that she had a lot going on and that she needed to deal with her issues. Rose was never fully attracted to him, so the break-up was an easy transition for her; however, Rose and Antonio stayed in communication despite her split with Marco. She and Antonio got close and discovered they were both attracted to the other.

It felt a bit awkward at first because of their connection through Marco, but Rose was drawn to Antonio in such a way she couldn't explain. She was transparent with Antonio concerning all what was going on in her life. He offered advice and sent her messages which helped in cheering her. His words were gentle; he showed great care for her. Rose had gotten to the point where she had forgotten that someone could care for her with such passion, even though they had never physically met. The issues she was facing did not throw him off; with him she felt she was not alone. He was interested in her and her life.

CHAPTER NINE

*Whoever oppresses the poor shows contempt
for their Maker, but whoever is kind to the
needy honors God.*

Proverbs 14;31 NIV

R ose was getting ready to move out of Elise's
home since she wanted some independence.
Elise was not happy about this. Rose noticed
Elise's mental condition was getting worse and suggested they visit a doctor together. Elise insisted it
would not be necessary since she had had the issue
from a young age. Although that claim made little sense,
there was so much going on in Rose's life that she didn't
push against it. She shrugged off her suspicion that Elise
was on drugs and instead refocussed on finalizing her
divorce, immigration status, and moving out.

Soon after, she received a letter from family court
saying the divorce was processed. She sighed: one thing

done—she was happy the divorce was finalized. Her contentment was short-lived as when she went to share the news with Elise, it was impossible to ignore just how "wired" her behavior was. Elise would be sleeping all day. It was when midnight came that she would get energized and start cleaning, doing laundry, and cooking. Rose stopped Elise just as she was about to run up the stairs again to put away more folded laundry. She held her by the shoulders and looked into her eyes. Elise squirmed, trying to avoid such direct eye contact.

"Elise, stop. What's really going on?"

Elise confessed she has been on drugs for the past two years and was currently trying to withdraw. The admission shocked Rose, even though it confirmed her suspicions. Rose was strongly against the use of recreational drugs, especially the type of drugs Elise disclosed she'd been using.

"Elise," Rose exclaimed. "These are the type of drugs that could eventually lead to you being on the streets, or dead from overdose!"

Elise dismissed her worries. "It's because I'm quitting without going into rehab, without professional help. That's probably why it's kind of more difficult," Elise said. I guessed that was why she was acting so abnormal.

Now it was out in the open, Rose couldn't believe she had not noticed everything sooner—she wished she had confronted Elise earlier. She had tried to convince Elise to attend church in the past, but Elise was not interested then nor now. Elise knew the life she was living was wrong in God's eyes and had no plans of converting. She preferred to stay away from church and claim her lifestyle was not sin in God's eyes.

"He would understand," Elise said.

Rose cared for Elise and wanted her safe and out of the dangers of drugs. She researched rehab clinics that would help her. Elise was subdued, no longer acting crazy. She was willing to be admitted at a rehab facility for support as withdrawal on her own was difficult and she wanted to get off the drugs. Rose found an affordable facility with a bed available and scheduled an intake tour knowing immediate action was necessary. Elise was in danger of going back to drugs, plus she was so ill due to withdrawal symptoms.

In the midst of all the challenges Rose was going through, she had to forgot about herself for a bit and became strong through helping her friend. It's like challenges just kept emerging one after the other. What kept Rose going was her faith in God, and her belief that He would make the end result a happy one for her and for those she loved.

Right around the time Elise was scheduled to be admitted to rehab, she began expressing how unhappy she was that Rose was soon moving out. Elise was worried about her business. She was concerned it would collapse with Rose's support while she was in rehab. Rose had assured Elise that she would come sleep over three days a week and continue to book the appointments every day.

Elise was still not placated. She wanted Rose at her house every day and pleaded with her even as they were packing her bags for her admittance to the facility. Emotions were high, but it was for the best, Rose kept reminding her. At the facility, Rose and Brian hugged Elise bye tearfully but they were all full of hope. Rose knew that when her friend got back after a month away, she would be back to her normal self and would be drug-use free.

The following night at around 11 pm, Rose was in bed and saw an incoming call from Elise. How could that be, she wondered. Elise was not allowed access to her phone while in rehab. Out of curiosity, she answered. It was Elise. Elise had convinced Brian to pick up her from the rehab facility.

Rose was furious. "How do you expect to fight your addiction? This is serious, Elise! It kills people. You have to stop using the drugs."

"I'll do it on my own," Elise replied. "That place was like prison. I couldn't take it."

"Ok," said Rose, then turned off her phone and had no trouble falling asleep. This was not a project she was willing to do more about at this time. She had researched and found Elise an exceptional and affordable rehab which Elise bailed from. Over the next week, Elise tried but was unable to draw Rose back into her situation. Rose did not allow Elise to distract her from her plans; instead it motivated her to move out completely and reduce her contact with Elise.

CHAPTER TEN

*You are my hiding place; you will
protect me from trouble and
surround me with songs of deliverance.*

Psalm 32:7 NIV

Rose had been in her new place about a month when Elise messaged her: there was a letter for her from immigration. Rose knew it was the letter she been expecting. Rose went to collect it, remembering that although the lawyers thought the chances of a successful appeal was slim, that if she received a second denial from immigration, it was okay. She would be eligible to appeal again.

After grabbing the letter from Elise, Rose was not eager to open it since she had focused her mind on not letting potential bad news discourage her. She got home and put the envelop on the table and considered what she would do if was denied. Was she ready to be disappointed again? She made a tea, trying to ignore the letter and build up the strength to open it. Sitting back at the table, she picked up the letter and held it up to the light. She tried to see if any clues were visible through the envelop. She knew that her hopes were very high although her chances of good news were low. She was not sure she could cope with more bad news.

Well, the answer was there—in that envelop, Rose reasoned. *It would not change whether she opened it now or two days from now.* She took a deep breath and tore open the envelop. She read the letter over and over to be certain she understood it properly. Her appeal was accepted. They granted her refugee status in Canada.

"Glory to God!" she screamed, then pushed back to get out of her chair. It clattered to the floor as Rose held her letter, jumping up and down and giving her thanks to God. With this acceptance, she was entitled to receive permanent residency in Canada. God had made possible what some lawyers thought was impossible. Rose immediately called Antonio to share. He was equally overjoyed with her news.

The following day Rose visited her lawyer to verify that she was free from the threat of deportation. He read the letter over and nodded, saying, "wow, this is rare." All that Rose could think was God had answered her prayer. She continuously thanked Him.

As the news sank in, Rose felt emotional. She had endured so much grief over the past years and finally got delivered from a major part of her stress. Once again, God had brought her out of a storm with victory— and without spousal sponsorship, which lawyers had claimed was the only possibility for her. He made a disappointment turn for her good.

This was more proof that with God, there is absolute hope. Rose had prayed and knew that God was able to do what she requested, her faith in Him made it possible. When no one, not even her lawyers thought she would have gotten accepted, God proved different.

At the moment Rose was still living just like a nonbeliever. She remembered her promise to change if she were allowed to stay in Canada. Rose planned on being born again but the question was when. She knew after receiving salvation she had to change her lifestyle completely otherwise it would not stand genuine with God. She had a boyfriend and was still helping at the spa.

That evening Rose received a call from an unrecognized number. Upon answering the call, the caller introduced herself as her ex-husband, Derek's, daughter. Rose found it strange that Derek's daughter was calling after a year. His daughter did not have good news:

she told Rose that Derek had passed away. A chill surrounded Rose upon hearing that. Her marriage with Derek did not work out, but she never imagined him being dead so soon. It took her a little while to absorb the news. She wondered how she would have managed if they were still married when he passed. But this didn't happen. They relationship was brief and ended long before this news. Rose learnt not to question the many possible outcomes. For her, things were now good. She confirmed her gratitude and blessings in prayers to God.

CHAPTER ELEVEN

Here I am! I stand at the door and knock. If anyone hears my voice and opens the door, I will come in and eat with that person, and they with me.

Revelation 3:20 NIV

Rose and Antonio fell in love with each other, connected only by phone and video calls. Now that Rose would be able to travel, they started to plan their first in-person date.

Marco was still in the dark about them. Rose and Antonio never thought they would have found love in this way, a love that brought such joy and happiness to them both. Antonio often sent her love songs letting her know the words described what he felt and how much she meant to him. Most of the songs left Rose speechless; he constantly amazed her in beautiful ways. The words in the songs and poems Antonio selected caused

Rose to feel his love from more than a thousand miles away. Rose and Antonio met when she was in the midst of a great life challenge. He stayed at her side, falling in love with her. When most people were running away from Rose due to the issues she was handling, Antonio chose to get closer to her.

That Antonio was a believer who devoted his Sundays to attending church pleased Rose. Sunday service had become more intense for her. While in congregation praising and worshipping, only she and the Lord knew what He had done for her. Only she knew what she had experienced, only she knew how grateful and thankful she was and would always be. Rose also knew she had to receive salvation and stick to living according to God's word, but her current situation was holding her back. Rose lived according to her senses and feelings. She felt that she had to be married first before being born again. She also knew she had to find another job. But with all the lawyer fees and bills, a minimum paying job would not cover her monthly bills. The thought of a minimum wage job with her huge bills scared her, but her current job was not aligned with her future with Christ. Rose applied to return to school. She knew that getting a solid good paying and legit job meant she needed to sharpen her education. She continued to bargain with God.

Rose obtained a student loan and worked in the evenings for Elise while attending college in the day. She

planned to continue working for Elise until she graduated and could get a good job. She really wanted out of
the appointment booking job but could not quit until
she had another means of paying her bills and support-
ing herself.

After a few months of school and working evenings,
Rose had located a church that increased her connection to God. The preaching was loaded and lead Rose to
some intense reflecting. A morning after school, Rose
was on the bus heading home when she ran into a lady
named Sue from the church. Sue shared there that there
was a global service lead by the ministry's head pastor
which was being broadcast live at the church and she
should come. That intrigued Rose. She stopped home
briefly then went to the service.

This was her first live service with this pastor. His
preaching and the messaged touch Rose in an amazing
way that nothing had ever touched her. Rose felt like
her heart was opened to receive God fully. Towards the
ending of the service the pastor directed a message to
whoever was listening and had not received salvation to
receive it now. This day Rose was ready. She did not care
about her huge bills and working a minimum wage job
while in school—she just knew it was time to receive
salvation and repent.

She repeated the words of the confession after
the pastor, believing the words with her heart. Rose

immediately felt different. There was this joy in her heart. She knew at this point there was no going back.

First thing she did after the service was quit her job. Secondly, she messaged Antonio and informed him that she had received salvation and given up the things that are not in line with God's commands and principles. She told him that fornication had to stop and she would no longer be visiting him in the US.

Rose used funds in her savings for her monthly bills while seeking a new job She never gave up faith in getting a part-time job even though she had been searching for months without securing one. Rose had complete faith in God. Things between Rose and Antonio had slowed down. He was acting cold with her, behaving like he was holding something back. Rose noticed that ever since she quit her job and got more involved with church, something had changed between them. She thought that was odd since Antonio was born again and actively engaged in his own church events.

She had expected her decision to make them closer. That it did not brought Rose grief. They had recently returned from vacation. Immediately after new year, Rose and Antonio had gone to Jamaica where Antonio was born and raised. They were planning their future together then he suddenly began treating her with disinterest. It had gotten to the point where almost anything she said would upset him, even asking why he was treating her this way would cause him to react in anger.

Rose began losing sleep; it got difficult to focus on her studies. She felt that Antonio wanted to dump her; she did not feel there was strength in her to overcome another heartbreak. She had grown to love him and felt love and passion that she never experienced before. She often prayed about it, but she felt she could not pray for someone to romantically want to continue a relationship with her, perhaps, especially one without premarital sex. She assumed the reason for his change in behavior was her unemployment and her deeper focus on living according to God's word. This confused her as she was not seeking financial assistance from him —she was using from her savings to get by.

She could not wrap her head around what was going on. Antonio who declared his genuine love for her, that he had never loved another as much as he loved her, began losing interest because she was jobless and wanted to obey God? She thought to herself that if someone truly loves another who becomes jobless mainly because she wants to live a life pleasing God, they will offer to help in any possible way. That was not the case with Antonio. Rose was attached to him. She loved him with all what made her alive, she didn't feel that she could manage if they were to break up.

Antonio showed Rose several pictures of a young lady who lived near him. It made the geographic distance between her in Canada and him on the other side of the border seem even greater. He claimed that the woman was interested in him and constantly sent him pictures of herself.

Rose suggested he block her number, but he responded that even though he did block her, the woman managed to send things to him through other means. This brought on more worries for Rose. Her boyfriend was acting cold and distant, and now he was sharing pics that another woman sent him. When she expressed concerns, Antonio said they cross paths through work and she often refers clients to him. Because of his job, he was reluctant to end all connections with her even though that is what Rose asked of him.

Rose then asked Antonio to not share the pics with her. He stopped but then, after only a few days, he sent her another one. She asked Antonio if he was sure he'd ask her to stop. Had he told the woman that he is in a relationship? He responded, yes. Rose then asked for her phone number. Antonio refused to give it to her, insisting he would take care of it.

But he didn't. Instead, Antonio was suddenly too busy with work to even have brief chats with her. When Rose brought it up and told him of the pain he was causing her, he dismissed her concerns and said he has made a decision to not have social calls during his work hours of nine in the morning to six in the evening. He said her constant nagging was turning him off.

From a loving and affectionate boyfriend, Antonio had turned into to a cold and tense one. Rose was already deeply attached. Even the thought of them breaking up brought her to tears. Rose had turned into this emotionally disturbed person, one she had avoided becoming despite all her problems in the past. She was always in tears; she had a constant dreaded in her about them breaking up. It was a pain she felt unable to endure. She would be on the train travelling from school and the thoughts of how Antonio had begun treating her would bring tears to her eyes. It felt too painful to hold back the tears even in public spaces. Rose felt helpless; she prayed and about it; but she was not sure what to ask of God since she could not pray someone into wanting to stay with her. She booked an appointment with a Christian therapist.

At the session she explained that she and Antonio had been going well and shortly after giving her life to Christ he began treating her differently. The therapist asked if she had discussed giving her life to Christ with her boyfriend before she did. Rose was stunned at such a question. She did not expect a Christian therapist to ask such a question. To Rose, giving her life to Christ needed no discussion. As far as she knew Antonio was a born-again Christian who she thought would be pleased that she had made that choice. The therapy session had no positive impact on what Rose was experiencing but she wondered why Antonio would not be pleased with her decision, even if she had not consulted him before making it.

When a guy from Rose's past began calling, she did not appreciate him it and brought it to Antonio's attention. Antonio asked Rose for his number. Rose responded that she had asked for the girl's number, yet he refused. Before she had even ended the sentence, Antonio disconnected the call. When Rose messaged him asking when he chose to act this way, he called her unpleasant and insulting names and said she should go be with that other guy. Rose was surprised Antonio thought so little of her.

CHAPTER TWELVE

*Trust in the LORD with all your heart and
lean not on your own understanding; in all
your ways submit to him, and
he will make your paths straight.*

Proverbs 3:5-6 NIV

Rose felt that she deserved an apology from Antonio. A week went by and things grew colder between them. While in conversation, Rose learnt that Antonio had no intention to apologize. She reflected on the past couple months with him, the constant pain due to how he was treating her and now the dirty words he used to describe her. Rose suggested to Antonio that perhaps they should go their separate ways. Antonio immediately agreed.

Rose should not have been surprised that he would be so quick to agree, but she was not serious. She did not want to break up. She stared at the phone and thought, *what have I done?* She called him, explaining she was not serious about breaking up, that she only said this because she has been feeling extremely hurt by the names he had called her.

Antonio explained that all of what was going on was on her. He accused her of not listening and not submitting to him. He also confirmed that he believed they should go their separate ways and that he had been thinking about it for some time. He told her that the next morning he would be travelling to Jamaica with Marco for a wedding and would not be available for a week.

Rose was curious as to why he never mentioned that trip sooner. His response was that they were not really in communication for the past week and that was when the sudden trip was planned.

Antonio supposedly departed that Friday morning and Rose refrained from calling over the weekend. The following Tuesday, Rose could not help it—she had not stayed this long without communicating with him since they started seeing each other. Antonio refused the calls telling her to move on with her life as he was doing the same. He sent a beach photo of the same girl who had signalled the trouble earlier. It was clear they were in Jamaica together on vacation.

This hit Rose like a wrecking ball. She was at school when he shared the picture and the news. She felt crushed and lost. How had everything changed so quickly? The man she loved and adored with all of her being, an experience she had never had, now hated her. Only a few weeks previous, they were making wedding plans and they had even talked of starting a family. He was no longer into her and was already with another woman.

Rose stayed in bed that evening and following day. She was not able to bring herself to eating, or even speaking. She'd shut down and was able to do nothing besides weep. She had a hard time wrapping her head around the way Antonio was treating her. The following day she messaged Antonio in disbelief that he had moved on so quickly.

If she did not get it the first time he said it, he called her and made it crystal clear. He told her that he was no longer in love with her, that he had moved on, and repeated that she should do the same. This time, Rose got it. She felt a bitter and sad wave of pain jolt through her entire body. She thought she was going to lose her sanity. She went back on her bed and did not move for a couple hours with her eyes wide open.

The following day, Rose kneeled in prayer seeking guidance from God. Rose had developed a habit of thanking God for her future husband that she believed would be Antonio. In this prayer, she was asking for strength to get over this heartbreak.

Rose could not prevent herself—she resumed messaging Antonio. He messages back and he kept saying that as time goes by, she would heal. He did not want messages of how much pain and lost she felt, saying he would block her number if she continued. Rose grieved heavily for a couple weeks and tried to stop thinking of him, but she could not. Rose messaged him again, letting him know that she was not ready to give up on him and their love. She felt stupid doing it, shameless even. But there was this feeling prompting her to it.

Despite his moving on Antonio was still having small talks with Rose. Rose would often stare at herself in the mirror and wonder what was wrong with her. Why couldn't she let him go? He clearly wasn't treating her as good as he should, but she was just trapped in the feeling she had for him. Without communication with him she felt sick and depressed. She was persistent in prayer seeking guidance and help from God.

A few weeks later, Antonio told Rose that the girl he was seeing was pregnant. "Why are you insisting on hurting me?" Rose asked. She felt that Antonio could have kept his news from until things calmed down. She was aware that he had moved on with her which was still painful. Him adding his new love was pregnant stung Rose, as he knew it would.

Rose knew that the only way out of this was her not being in love with him. She relied on God to wipe off what she felt for Antonio, but it was just not happening. She was still deeply in love with Antonio. Rose placed focus on getting over Antonio. She made herself busier. She got involved in the church ministry and joined the choir. She attended regional and local services and choir activities. She and Antonio were still in communication though. Being completely cut off from him brought her too much pain.

A few weeks after the news of Marco expecting a child, his mother, who lived in Canada, passed away. Antonio planned to travel to Canada and shared the details with Rose. Rose felt like she wanted to see him, perhaps a last time. When she suggested the meeting, he agreed. Rose immediately booked a train ticket to Montreal. That evening while Rose was waiting for Antonio to arrive, she planned everything she would say to his face. The last time Antonio and Rose were together, she had not been born again. Rose planned on having a heartfelt and honest conversation with Antonio.

When he walked into the foyer, he reached out for a hug, and Rose accepted. While she was letting go, he kissed her. Antonio was tied up with funeral functions which meant he and Rose saw little of each other. The morning they were heading back to their homes, Antonio told Rose that he loved her.

Rose met Antonio for some closure, but things had gotten more complicated. Antonio had gotten this woman he supposedly moved on with pregnant and now he was telling Rose he still loved her? His declaration of love was exactly what Rose had dreamed of—what she wanted to hear—but she hadn't truly expected it and now what was she to do in such a situation? They had spoken about having a child and now another woman was carrying his child. Rose kept asking herself why it had to be her experiencing something so messy. Why were all those painful issues pursuing her?

CHAPTER THIRTEEN

*Dear friends, do not be surprised at the
fiery ordeal that has come on you to test you,
as though something strange were
happening to you.*

1Peter 4:12 NIV

At that point nothing could surprise Rose. She had been hit in all different directions and trusted that God had joy prepared for her at some point. She felt certain that Antonio was her future husband and believed this episode with this other woman was to test their love. Antonio told Rose that he would not continue with the woman, that he wanted them to get back together. Rose asked his plan regarding his child she was carrying. He response was that he would care for the child.

That was not the life Rose had in mind. Regardless, she loved him and did not want a life without him.

As weeks went by Rose and Antonio reconciled; they avoided conversations about his soon-to-be-born child.

Rose had opened up to a friend about what she had been through with Antonio. After sharing the friend's opinion with him, Antonio was displeased she had told someone. He claimed that he had not gone on vacation with another woman and that he was never actually seeing anyone else. The moving on and baby story were his way of ending their relationship since he believed Rose was not listening to his requests. Rose was shocked though relieved by his revelation. She was hurt that he made up this heart-wrenching story just to end their relationship. But Antonio stood strong with the choices he made and had no remorse for what it had brought on Rose.

But what about the photograph of him and the girl on vacation in Jamaica? Rose thought. But she decided not to ask her question as things were already too difficult and confusing. She did want the relationship between her and Antonio to work itself out.

As time went by, Rose tried to wrap her head around the entire made-up story and the pain and depression she experienced. She could not understand why he allowed her to endure so much when he could have ended it with the truth. Antonio's reason was that he really wanted out of the relationship since she refused to obey his requests. Rose was unconditionally in love with a man who would allow her to be in pain for many months. In her mind she wanted to break up with him, but she was deeply in love and being without him in her life brought sadness.

As their relationship progressed Antonio made plans to visit Rose. However, when the date got close, he cancelled. Rose suspected that he intentionally delaying the progress of the relationship, but Rose chose to believe what he told her. Antonio also made it seem like Rose's attitude proved she was not fully ready for the next step in their relationship. This went on month after month, with him setting, then cancelling, plans to see her.

He then had Rose wearing an engagement ring on her index finger to make a public statement that she was not available and in a committed relationship. He called it a commitment ring, not an engagement ring which was why he insisted she wear it on her index versus ring finger. Rose did as he requested. He called on video when she was out to verify that she was, indeed, wearing the ring and that it was on the correct finger. Rose was patient with Antonio, they were both getting deeper in God's word and making plan for a future together. They sometimes shared messages from different pastors and discussed scriptures. Based on the statements made by Antonio, Rose got the impression the next time they met he would propose. She grew convinced of this. They had agreed on having a child and since they were both devoted to living a life pleasing God, Antonio kept making comments that he would have his brother be his best man.

As Rose got more wrapped in God's word certain conversations and jokes (like those about sex) were no longer of interest to her. This sometimes caused hiccups with Antonio. She knew which direction she wanted to head; she also knew that fornication was not an act she was willing to repeat. Antonio made various statements which lead her to believe he was also ready for marriage.

Rose completed school and graduated with distinction. God had blessed her with a good job immediately after graduation. Her thirtieth birthday was approaching, and Antonio had promised to visit her before it. This would be followed by another trip. When her birthday came, she would travel to New York City to see him. The time approached but Antonio made no move to visit her. They changed their plan. Instead, Rose to travel to him to celebrate her birthday and then, two weeks afterwards, he would visit her in Toronto.

In the days leading to her trip, they were both excited. The night before travelling Rose was not pleased that the three-day trip had cost her way more than expected. When she mentioned this, he got upset and told her to cancel the trip even though she was not, of course, suggesting she did not want to visit him. He got upset about her choice of words. As the flight and hotel was non-refundable, Rose ignored his request and said she was still headed there. If he chose not to meet her at the airport, she would just make her way to the hotel solo.

The following morning while Rose was travelling Antonio refused her calls and ignored the messages. On arrival at the airport, she received a message from him informing that he was outside waiting. That messaged cheered her up. She was excited and happy to see him after a year. When Rose entered Antonio's car, he played tense for a few minutes then softened up. While grabbing lunch and hanging out, all the hiccups and cancelled trips were forgotten.

However, Rose had recently got a haircut which Antonio was fine with until they were together. She had been facing challenges with her scalp, likely due to stress, which caused hair loss on various parts of her head. Antonio was extremely focussed on how she looked, saying her looks made him feel uncomfortable being in public with her. Usually, Rose's hair looked spectacular. Rose was self-conscious about her hair and felt unhappy when see noticed Antonio's attitude. He refused to take pictures with Rose, and she gave up her hopes that the trip would go well.

On many occasions Rose suggested to Antonio that when they get together, they should hold hands in prayer and commit themselves before God as a couple. Rose believed if they blessed their relationship in prayer and presented themselves to God as husband and wife, He would not judge their intimacy as fornication. Antonio would not consider the idea, which seemed odd to her since he too was a born again and baptized son of God. Anytime Rose brought up the topic, Antonio would ignore it. Rose had dedicated her life completely so she could be in the right standing with God's commands and principles. She did not want to be fornicating. That she made clear to Antonio, but he pretended he was not hearing her.

Later that evening while at dinner, Rose noticed Antonio was seated facing away from her while on his phone playing games. She asked whether he would get off the phone and face her. Antonio responded that he is a grown man and does how he please. That response right there revealed a lot to Rose.

While sitting in a restaurant with her boyfriend she had not seen for over a year his focus was not on her. She excused herself for some air. Rose felt beyond overwhelmed. She could not stop herself from tearing up. It was clear to her that Antonio no longer wanted to be with her. She knew that part of it had to do with him feeling embarrassed of her hair and her persistence about God's commands.

All she knew was that she travelled to spend her birthday with the man she been planning a life with, a man she loved unconditionally who was presently treating her like someone he did not want to be with. This launched a dark cloud of pain over her, especially as based on the statements and plans Antonio claimed he was making, Rose had believed he would be proposing on the trip. When she realised that things were heading in the opposite direction, her heart grew heavy. When they returned to the resort it was midnight, marking Rose's birthday. Antonio gifted her with a beautiful bag and gift set. She was grateful and showed him appreciation. Although this was not how Rose thought it would turn out, but she was thankful for the gifts.

The next morning the energy was not cheerful between them. Rose was still feeling the effects of how Antonio reacted while at dinner and the comments he made suggested he was not ready for the next step in their relationship. They had been in a long-distance relationship for over two years, making plans for a family. While at the pool they got into conservation about their future. Antonio stated that Rose needed to change and that it was *she* who was not ready for marriage.

His words hit her strongly, as for the past two years she made drastic changes in her life for him in response to his requests. It hit her that whatever she did, even how she carried herself, was never enough for Antonio. He constantly found faults in her. The slightest mistakes she made would be blown up into a huge matter by him. Antonio was intentionally delaying things between them for a reason she couldn't think of. She felt extremely overwhelmed and could not control her tears from falling as they sat by the pool.

The tears made Antonio furious. He was concerned that people would see her. Rose felt tired. She was tired of trying to please a man who was really not on the same page as her. She had invested over two years of her life in this long-distance relationship, placing her trust in it, and here on her birthday the man she loved unconditionally was bringing her down with his words. It was like he was Mr. Perfect and Rose was a big mess-up.

When evening came, he took her for dinner at a five-star restaurant. Rose, who was in a fragile state, began tearing up. Antonio was turned off; she could not help crying and excused herself, going to the ladies' room. The trip was a disaster.

The following morning while getting prepared to head home, Antonio was speaking about the trip he had planned to make to visit Rose in a couple weeks. His initial plan was solely to spend time with Rose, but now he said, the main point of the trip was to attend a wedding. Rose had always noticed the dishonesty in Antonio, but she avoided mentioning his lies to keep peace. This was a challenge she had with him; he often lied and she pretended he had not. Rose got the feeling that she would not be seeing him again. She figured it was over and he was no longer interested.

CHAPTER FOURTEEN

But when he, the Spirit of truth, comes, he will guide you into all the truth. He will not speak on his own; he will speak only what he hears, and he will tell you what is yet to come.

John16:13 NIV

Back at home Rose focussed on moving forward. It had been a painful past year with Antonio, who stood her up, month after month and when they finally got together, he was a changed man. In her mind she wanted to be cut off from him, but she felt deeply emotionally attached. When Antonio told Rose that he was considering another trip with her to analyze what went wrong, Rose felt shamelessly happy and agreed. Antonio had decided on the dates he would visit, but as usual, when the date arrived, he made an excuse, telling her an urgent business trip came up. A few days later, he gave a different the reason for cancelling the trip. He was telling a lie.

This time Rose confronted him about the different stories and, as was typical, Antonio shut down Rose and accused her of not trusting him. Rose was confused, wondering if Antonio did not remember he had shared conflicting reasons for his business trip. Antonio felt Rose needed to apologize but Rose was sure of his dishonestly despite how firmly he was standing with it. Rose thought to herself that this was not the type of man she wanted to spend her life with. Still, she was not ready to end things.

The following week, Antonio told Rose he would be in China for five days on business, so Rose did not message him since she did not want to cause roaming charges to be added to his cellphone bill. When he was supposedly back from the trip he rejected her calls, and even went as far as blocking her number. She had accepted that he no longer wanted to be with her, but the mountain ahead was the reality that she would have to learn to fall out of love with him.

While scrolling through Instagram, Rose stumbled across on a photo of Antonio's supposedly ex-wife. She felt it was odd it would cross her feed and she examined the photo and noticed Antonio in the background. The dates matched the date of his sudden trip to China for business. Finally, the truth. Even though they were no longer together, it was a relief to have proof he had lied to her. He had been at a resort with his supposedly ex-wife. She'd had her suspicions but now here was proof. He was back with his ex-wife.

At first Antonio pretended he did not know what Rose was referring too. She sent him the pic of the time he claimed to be in China on business but was actually at a resort in Florida where he lives, with his supposedly ex. Antonio realised he could not lie anymore and asked Rose not to jump into conclusions until he called and to explain.

His explanation was that as he got deeper in God's word, he realised that a man cannot divorce his wife and remarry. Rose then asked him why he lied to her all this time, letting her believe he was not married. Antonio responded his initial plan was to finalize things with his ex and get married to Rose.

During their relationship Antonio, had Rose believe he was residing in the same house as his aunt and cousin. This was a untrue. He was living with his wife. Their daughter was away at university. Rose had been in a relationship with a married man. Antonio was a believer and engaged in duties at church. Antonio was not who he pretended to be.

Upon meeting Antonio, she opened up to him about the past abuse she endured. That did not stop him from deceiving her and bringing her into a relationship built on lies. Who would believe a man portraying himself as a dedicated Ambassador for God's Kingdom would have the desire to put a woman through this? A woman who he knew had endured hurt and abuse from another ex?

Rose was speechless and got lost in the light which was just shed upon her. She was clearly in darkness with Antonio. God had brought her into the light. This explained the on and off behavior she experienced with Antonio throughout the time she thought he was her man. He actually spoke about kids and agreed on names despite knowing that it was all a fake relationship.

Rose gave thanks to God for bringing her in the light. She felt like a weight had been lifted off her life: she saw Antonio for who he clearly was. That was not from God; he was provoked by an evil spirit. He needed help. She thought to herself that no woman should have to go through this. She had invested part of her life in a relationship with a man who was not who she thought, who constantly saw faults in her while he was living a double life. He tried to change her and had comments and input in all she did when all along he was not honest about his life. Rose had just spent three years of her life with a man she did not know at all. A man who at one point requested she wear an engagement ring because he saw her as his fiancé.

Rose accepted the disappointment by enduring the pain it brought, having faith that God would turn her despair into joy. She also asked God for forgiveness for being in a relationship with a married man. God knew that Rose was unaware of Antonio's true life; He knew her heart. This gave Rose courage to rejoice since she had the right intentions in heart and felt taken advantage of.

Rose had moments where she would break down and other times where she was giving God praise for delivering her from this man. After a few of those episodes, Rose finally made the decision to put great effort into finding God's purpose for her life and not allowing what the devil did to get in the way.

PART II

God's Plans for Us

CHAPTER FIFTEEN

The Spirit of the Lord is upon me, and he has anointed me to be hope for the poor, healing for the broken-hearted, and new eyes for the blind, and to preach to prisoners, You are set free! I have come to share the message of the Jubilee, for the time of God's great acceptance has begun.

Luke 4:18,19 TPT

Many women experience malicious deceit and domestic abuse which scars them emotionally. Those scars often lead to loosing hope in life and choosing to continue dark paths because they feel there is nothing better for them. This is because of heartbreak and terrible treatment the devil has used men to bring about.

With the mixture of the challenges Rose faced between the age of nineteen to thirty years, without God in her life, she could have led down a path of destruction.

Putting her trust in our living God and his ability to give her peace and success, Rose prevailed. Those hardships empowered her to fulfill a life of great purpose.

This young lady also battled unexplained hair loss. Doctors diagnosed her with alopecia. In beginning she felt scared and tried different products to fight it. When she got in God's word and discovered that Jesus was wounded for our transgressions, He was bruised for our iniquities; The chastisement for our peace was upon him. And by his stripes we are healed. (Isaiah 53:4-5) She also discovered that being a new creature in Christ Jesus she should never be sick or ill. Everything is possible for the one who believes. (Mark 9:23)

Fear in Rose was gone. With those scriptures Rose confessed that she has the life of God. She spoke to her scalp and declared that it will produce strong and healthy hair with the faith that it would. She had received discouraging comments claiming that her hair would not grow back. Her response was that her faith in God will cause her hair to grow strong and healthy. Being in Christ Jesus her hair ought to grow strong and healthy.

Thankfully our loving God is faithful to us who seek and worship him in truth, he turns our despair into joy. God is able to do exceedingly abundantly above all that we ask or think according to the power that is at works in us.

When the word of God is not constant in our lives and hardship comes, we endure excessive grief. Without knowing that we can cast all our cares on God and He will mend our hearts, we feel like our existence is useless. The devil tries to cause us to believe that we can't overcome the situations. A heart break from someone who you planned a life with can bring you feel that you can't be happy without that person. It will ruin months of your life simply because the pain in your emotions hinders you from letting go. You may no longer want to be with that person, but the devil will use your emotions to distract you from being healed.

We often question why the constant betrayal and heartache. This is all the work of the devil who is always trying to get us to believe that life is filled with grief and some of us are cursed. The devil knows that persons living without the Holy Spirit are targets to joining his evil kingdom. He will use the mistakes made to have people believe they are bad. When someone has the mentality that they are bad, then all efforts to do good are lost. They naturally feel unhappy and depressed, pushing them towards drugs and other sinful activities to distract them from the depression. They become scared of themselves since the devil makes them feel shameful and worthless. If only they knew and believed the devil was responsible for this and he's a liar, that God is ready to forgive and restore a life of peace and joy.

When the devil gets in the mind of one, he uses that person to hurt another, then he expects the hurting person to start doing his acts. The devil uses one person to cause pain to the next so his works can be spread all over. Stories like Rose's are a testimony that the devil cannot prevail where God's Spirit dwells. The devil made countless attempts to destroy this young lady, but God was with her. Rose was in the position to choose a life hating people for causing her grief but with God in her life she understood it was the work of the devil. The devil used people to hurt her. She chose to forgive and love all who had hurt and used her.

God created man to dominate and prosper on earth. God does not create anything with the intention for it to fail. We were all created to dominate in an area with excellence. Our Father in heaven is a creator of excellence. We all should acknowledge we carry a beautiful purpose and live conscious of our inheritance in Christ our Savior. Our inheritance is the Kingdom of God. Christ came to restore it on Earth. It should be our lifestyle to be obedient to his commands and principles along with earnestly seeking his will.

When Adam ate the fruit, he lost God's Spirit which dwelled in he and Eve. They also lost access to God's kingdom. This was passed along to every other human who was born. Men were solely living by flesh. After

Jesus died and was rose from the grave, he returned that access to man.

We receive the Spirit of God in us by accepting Jesus as our Lord and Savior with confession and faith in him. Therefore, with the Spirit of God dwelling in us we are able to achieve all what is good and most of all we have access to eternal life. We no longer live by the flesh but by the Holy Spirit. Being aware that the Spirit of God dwells in us we ought to live in right standing with him to have continuous access to living in his Divine Kingdom. It's God's will for us to reign on earth in the invisible Kingdom Jesus brought. In God's Kingdom all our needs are supplied, there is no sickness, lack, depression, or disease. We have a life of restoration. The time here on Earth is to pursue and fulfill God's purpose until our Lord returns to select the elect. We qualify for eternal life based on how that time is used.

CHAPTER SIXTEEN

Peace I leave with you; my peace I give you.
I do not give to you as the world gives.
Do not let your hearts be troubled and
do not be afraid.

John 14:27 NIV

The process of recovering from hurt and abuse to living the divine life is a journey that one must commit to. It takes discipline and the hunger to fulfill God's purpose for creating you. The number one distraction could be our thoughts and the memories of the past.

Letting go of a life lived and plans made especially when it involves a relationship, a future, is a battle. As much as we may want to forget the memories or that person, our thoughts and dreams struggle against that. Thankfully discovering God's plan for us is always greater and sets us on a path to peace and happiness.

Yes, we may sometimes feel that there could have been happiness with the person we had to say goodbye to. But the reality is that we can only be truly happy when living the life God predestined for us. Once we come to realise this, strength and courage comes, allowing us to move on.

During this transformation our emotions may struggle. There are days where we feel in control and not distracted by the emotions of heartbreak. Whereas on another day we may feel miserable and the hurtful as the breakup clouds us. One the days where the paining emotions surface, we need to remind ourselves of what God has shown us for the future. The joy of his plan is far happier and fulfilling than what we thought was our happiness.

The devil will become more persistent, trying our emotions to cause setbacks when we have decided to live righteous and seek God's purpose. God's plan for us is good and not for failure. He did not create us for unhappiness and failure but to succeed and live prosperous. This is why it is very important to always stay connected to God. This enables us to experience all what he planned for each day we walk the face of the earth, allowing us to let go of the past and move into the divine life. Having faith in God and believing the visions He showed us shall come to pass. Without faith in God and the certainty that what He has shown shall happen, we miss out on it. God shows us His plans but our faith in Him makes it happen.

How hungry are you for genuine love, joy, peace, success, and prosperity? There is no love greater and more satisfying than the love of God.

Think about it this way: when we feel hunger pangs, we rely on the food eaten to suppress that hunger. Certain food choices may carry ingredients that are not nutritious which can lead to disadvantages in the functioning of the body and will only keep the stomach filled for a short period. There are also other options which contains nutritious ingredients which will excellently aid in the body functioning and will suppress the hunger for an extended period.

Likewise, when we are hungry for a life of prosperity and joy, we ought to eat the right foods and engage in the activities which will produce lasting results. The right foods will aid in our development and give us lasting joy, peace, and happiness. This is why we out to start off with God and his Word. In him we are complete, and he supplies all the food we require for reaching our joyful goals.

Once we've let go of a certain lifestyle, we are given the opportunity to start a new chapter. It is very important that we start with a source who is reliable and guarantees joy. The Lord Jesus is that only source.

When overcoming heart break, the devil will try to introduce many unrighteous methods which gives a temporary ease. They may seem like the easy way out because you are eager to get rid of the pain. The easy unrighteous way will only lead you deeper into darkness which will double the pain when it crashes. And yes, it will crash. Anything that's not built of righteousness (right standing with God) will eventually fall. Anyone who has suffered continuous hurt and makes up their mind to take control and not fall back into that same sinkhole should choose righteousness. That's the only way to experience lasting peace and joy.

Once you have come to accept this truth, the devil gets scared. He knows that he's losing and no longer has access to hurting or using you. He knows that you have seen his works and won't allow him to use you for his dirty desires. Bear in mind this will not prevent him from placing temptation in your paths—temptations you will walk over as long as you stay connected to your source, our loving God. You must also believe that you can achieve all you want—that it can happen--before it does happen. For with God, we operate by faith. Making the decision to set focus on discovering the true happiness God has prepared for you must include you trusting him completely by seeing no possibility in reviving the past. Giving thanks to him for all he has done and trusting his plans for you shall come to pass. Completely relying on him has to be backed up with your way of life. The decisions that you make have to be in lined with his principles; your mood should be more cheerful because you are expecting great things.

You will face situations with a confident a positive perspective, because you know that you are in God's care and things are working for your good. You start being more kind and more welcoming to people around you, especially those who may have hurt you in the past. You know that you are on route to discovering your true happiness, so past disappointments no longer get to you.

Once you have accepted that God created you for great purpose and you set focus on discovering that purpose, your entire being should be transformed to living for God. You can accomplish nothing successful that lasts without Him. Note I said "lasts" meaning that it will never perish. Even when we are recalled and our spirit departs the Earth, what we have accomplished through him goes with us. Our great reward is after we have departed the Earth. Works that are done without God perishes.

Rose experienced massive heartbreaks along with mistreatment from people she cared for. When this young lady believed she finally met her life partner, three years later, she found out he was still married. Rose could have chosen to allow the pain and disappointments of the past twelve years weigh her down. She could have continued on a path of life with no meaning, just living each day as it comes. Thankfully to God she dismissed that thought and made the decision not to let those past years prevent her from experiencing the joy God predestined. She trusted God to eliminate those emotions which brought pain. Rose made up her mind to discover God's purpose for creating her. She started reading the Bible daily, to mediate on Scriptures and was happy to discover that the more she read, more was revealed. As her knowledge increased, her emotions began to heal. This gave her confidence that she would soon be entering new doors of joy.

Rose started having visions. It took her a few days before understanding what it meant, but when she received the revelation, focus was placed on achieving it. She invested time into messages on how to manage visions from God.

Rose mediated on the scriptures:

"A man's heart plans his way, But the Lord directs his steps".

"And we know that all things work together for good to those who love God, to those who are called according to his purpose.

She wrote the visions and a plan to achieve them. Rose was confident and happy about her new journey with the Holy Spirit.

As Rose mediated and took in God's word she became at peace. The emotional pain she had been carrying was gone. She thanked God for removing that painful cloud within her. Rose began feeling one hundred percent good on the inside. Even though the thought of Antonio popped up now and again, she no longer felt the hurt and disappointment. She discovered what was ahead would bring far more joy than the hurt she endured.

God is truly love and proves it day after day. He is the answer to all what we face in life. His love and mercy for us washes all pain away. We only have to trust in Him.

Rose envisioned herself fulfilling the visions God showed her. As she mediated on His word, she received greater faith that it was going to happen. Her visions were bigger than she imagined; they made her realise why the devil had been after her. The devil knew that God had great plans for her which would extend God's Kingdom here on Earth—that is why the devil tried to derail her.

Rose began sharing her plan with a few people. Some took her seriously whereas others gave feed-back which indicated they did not really believe she would accomplish her goals. Rose had finally found her heart's desire. She wanted to be a positive influence and to do the work God had given desire for.

For a first time in over twelve years Rose's was finally at peace. The peace in her heart felt extremely sweet. This was all God's doing. He had given her a new song to sing.

I am no longer in pain.

I no longer live in fear.

I no longer tear with emotional pain.

I no longer feel confused.

I've found peace.

I'm in the light,

All thanks to God for his love and mercy.

Rose saw God's favour on her. Immediately after graduating from school, Rose found a good job. Close to a year later, when she decided to change jobs for an increase in pay, she got a new job with exactly what she desired within three months. Rose continuously gives praise and thanks to God for flowing blessings into her life.

Rose looked back and thought of the different directions which do not include relying on God, directions she could have been tempted to head to when in grief. She realised that many other women around the world endure abuse and hurt and could use her example to stand strong and head towards God. So many have experience worse than she has and are tempted in the wrong directions. There are those who got provoked in being violent during abuse and betrayal. They are currently spending their lives behind bars, all because of a wrong decision led by grief. There are women roaming the streets using drugs to numb that internal pain which was led by heartbreak and abuse.

We have sisters living with guilt as bondage, all because of wrong choices made during their youth. Shame and guilt are literally eating them on the inside. The list can go on with all the fallings being a result of abuse and heartbreak.

Rose felt compassion for those women. She wanted to lead them to God. Letting them know that God is ready to forgive them, that a life with him brings divine joy and content. Rose developed the desire to help bring them out of the bondage of hurt and guilt. She wanted those women to find joy like she found in God. Just as God healed her from the past twelve years of hurt and abuse, she knew God was able to do much more for others.

Many women go through those life-sucking situations in silence and feel too embarrassed to share. There's this feeling of being judged by others, especially family members and close colleagues. Sometimes they feel too ashamed to share what they deal with behind closed doors. The one who sees everything is God. He loves all and is always there when we seek Him. He is able to bring break all bondages and set those who seek Him free. Jesus has made the way to God. Confessing the Lordship of Jesus Christ and asking for forgiveness of sins gives access to a life of rest. There is hope for everyone who turns to Christ. Depending completely on God's will can bring you out of that darkness which encases them in pain from hurt and scars from betrayal. God will cause you to flourish. The first step in coming out of this bondage is to trust that God has already done it.

If you had not received salvation, you do that immediately as that will then connect you spiritually to Christ. The moment that Christ dwells in you, all things become possible. You now have access to the Kingdom of God. In God's Kingdom, there is no pain, no heartbreak, no feeling of rejection, no sickness, no disease. In God's Kingdom there is joy, hope, faith, love, and eternal life.

Salvation Prayer

Heavenly Father, I believe with my heart that Jesus Christ is the Son of the living God. I believe that he died for me, and God raised Him from the dead. I believe He's alive. I confess with my mouth that Jesus Christ is the Lord of my life. I have eternal WHAT; I am born again. I am a child of God. Thank you, Lord, for saving my soul.

ACKNOWLEDGEMENTS

I would like to thank and acknowledge the Holy Spirit for bringing out this book. He strengthened me and guided me in its writing.

A wonderful thank you to Pastor Tabatha Pena for her contribution in the structuring my story. I also thank Akosua Joy Brown and her team at What's Your Story – Author Services. Wow, thank you so much for every bit of work and effort invested in the publishing of this book.

Finally, to all readers: a sincere thank you for choosing to read it.

ABOUT THE AUTHOR

Deanva Stephen hails from Christ and is passionate about the Gospel of Christ. She was born and raised on a small Caribbean island of the Helen of the West, Saint Lucia. She migrated to Canada in her early adult years and now lives in Toronto, Ontario. Deanva loves baking, a gift she's been blessed with.

Therefore, if anyone is in Christ,
the new creation has come:
The old has gone, the new is here!
2Corinthians 5:17